ANDREA JAEGER, TENNIS CHAMPION

Also by Julianna A. Fogel and Mary S. Watkins:
Wesley Paul, Marathon Runner

ANDREA JAEGER
TENNIS CHAMPION

by Julianna A. Fogel and Mary S. Watkins

J. B. Lippincott   New York

Our thanks to the Jaeger family—Roland, Ilse, Susy, and Andrea—for sharing their world with us. Also, our thanks to our families, for their loving support.

Designed by Kohar Alexanian

First Edition

Library of Congress Cataloging in Publication Data
Fogel, Julianna A.
     Andrea Jaeger, tennis champion.
     SUMMARY: Highlights the life of 14-year-old
Andrea Jaeger, youngest tennis pro ever, who began
playing tennis at age 8 and entered her first
tournament at 9.
     1. Jaeger, Andrea—Juvenile literature.
2. Tennis players—United States—Biography—
Juvenile literature. [1. Jaeger, Andrea.
2. Tennis players] I. Watkins, Mary S.
II. Title.
GV994.J33F63   796.342′092′4 [B] [92]
ISBN 0-397-31915-0   79-9619
ISBN 0-397-31916-9 (lib. bdg.)

1 2 3 4 5 6 7 8 9 10

To Curt, for his ace ideas
and
To Jerry, for claiming "take-backs"

I'm Andrea Jaeger.
I'm fourteen, and tennis is a big
part of my life right now. I've
been playing since I was eight.

When I first started playing tennis, my dad threw balls to me in the driveway. He wouldn't take me on a court until I was strong enough to hit the ball over the net. Our garage still has grease marks on the door where I used to practice hitting.

I thought tennis was fun, but I don't think I would have stuck with it if it hadn't been for my dad. He told me, "Andrea, I think you have natural talent. You can be a good player, maybe even a champion. But you have to work at it."

Dad is a pro. He coaches me and my older sister, Susy. Susy is seventeen, and she is a competitive player also. Mother used to play, but she says she's too busy now just keeping up with our schedules.

I'm kind of a tomboy. At school I'm on a relay team, and I've won ribbons every year at field day.

My dad taught me how to play soccer. I used to play sweeper position on a boys' team, but the games were held at the same time as my tennis tournaments, so I had to quit.

I love to ride my bike, but sometimes when my friends ask me to go on a bike ride or to a movie, I can't because I have to practice tennis. My friends understand.

It seems like a lot of good tennis players live in either
California or Florida. We live in Chicago, where the weather
makes it impossible to play tennis outdoors all year.

In the wintertime, Susy and I practice on the indoor
courts where my dad teaches. We play three hours after
school every day and five hours a day on the weekends.

My dad is always coming up with new drills. There are drills for everything: forehands, backhands, lobs, overheads.

He has us play right up near the net and hit volleys. We try to keep the ball in play—at least thirty hits each—without letting it bounce.

Sometimes he has us concentrate on hitting crosscourt shots, or we might work on placing balls in certain corners of the court.

One drill that is murder is "two against one"—when Susy and my dad team up and hit shots to me. The drill is good for developing speed and anticipation, but it's hard because you have to keep moving all the time.

Sometimes we serve and play out points. I always keep track of how many points I win, but they're never as many as Susy's. Whenever I get impatient racing all over the back of the court hitting ground strokes, I always move up to the net. I like going to the net. I'm not afraid of getting hit by the ball, but I worry when I hit a short ball to Susy, because she can really smash those shots past me!

When I was nine, I entered my first tournament and won. Most tournaments have age divisions, like twelve years and under, fourteen and under, sixteen and under, eighteen and under. Since I was twelve, my national ranking has been number one for my age division.

When I was thirteen and had won so many tournaments, we had a family meeting and decided I could start playing in an older age division. My parents also decided that Susy and I were old enough to start traveling to tournaments by ourselves.

8

When we pack for a tournament, we each take three pairs of tennis shoes. We wear out a pair a week when we play on hard courts. Once I had to finish playing a match with a hole right through both my sock and shoe.

Susy and I each pack five graphite racquets. That sounds like a lot, but once Susy broke two in one day. We try not to favor a particular racquet in case it should break, but it's hard not to get used to one grip that's more comfortable than the others.

When we're playing a tournament doubles match, Susy always serves first, since she's the stronger server and I'm better playing net. We play totally different types of games. Susy likes to stay back and hit ground strokes. She's willing to wait all day for her opponent to make a mistake. Not me! I get impatient. I have to force myself to stay back from the net.

It bothers me if I feel we're being cheated out of a point. If I think I'm right, I won't budge. Sometimes it seems to me that Susy's so nice, she almost *gives* points away.

We never argue between points. If one of us makes a mistake, the other one says something encouraging. If I hit a shot and it lands out, Susy might say, "That's okay, nice try."

Susy and I make a good doubles
team because we play together
so much. Sometimes our opponents
underestimate us. They think
that because I'm little, we won't
be a strong team. But we are
ranked number one nationally in
doubles in the sixteen-and-under
division.

Susy and I aren't always partners. We have ended up
playing against each other eight times in tournaments. Susy
says that when she plays me, she's more relaxed and
confident than she is against any other player. Even though
I try to play the ball and not the person, when I look across
the net and see Susy, I lose every time.

Reporters are always asking if there's any jealousy or rivalry between Susy and me, because I've received so much publicity. There's no jealousy. Susy plays with me so much, we both feel she's a part of every match I win. And when I lose, she's the one who can cheer me up best.

Between matches, Susy tries to get me to practice with her. She even tries to get me to jump rope, which is supposed to be good for your footwork. I tell her that I'm plenty agile and that soccer's better than jumping rope—besides, I'd rather watch TV or play cards.

We call home every night when we're away at tournaments. When we win, my dad wants to know the scores. Sometimes, if my opponent wasn't a strong player, he says, "You shouldn't have lost so many games, Andrea."

We've learned not to make excuses. Instead, we try to tell him what our weaknesses were so that when we get home, we can work on them. If I feel down because I lost, he reminds me, "You learn more from losses than you do from wins."

Right after my eighth-grade graduation last spring, Susy and I began hitting on an old, cracked court near our house. I was trying to get used to hitting balls that would bounce in funny, unexpected ways because my next tournament was going to be played on grass.

I was going to England, to play at Wimbledon.

Every tennis player dreams of playing at Wimbledon someday. Tennis tournaments have been held there for over one hundred years. I was invited to play in Junior Wimbledon. I would be playing against the best junior players from over thirty countries.

I started practicing six hours a day. That much practice can get grueling. But when I practice hard, then go into a tough match and win over somebody who's good—maybe somebody I couldn't have beaten before—I know it's been worth all those hours.

Susy and I also began to work with a pro, Steve Casati. He explained how playing on grass is different from playing on clay or hard courts. On clay, the balls play slow. On hard courts, they play fast. On grass, not only do the balls play fast, but every bounce is different. Even special heavier balls are used.

Most important, grass courts are slippery and uneven, and it's hard for players to move quickly on them. So Steve had me concentrate on moving and footwork. Over and over, I practiced standing at the back fence, running up, then getting set before hitting the ball.

Mom went with me to Wimbledon. Susy had a tournament in Texas, and Dad had to stay in Chicago to teach. I wished they could have come along, too.

There are now eighteen courts at Wimbledon. The most important matches are played in Court One and Center Court. It was really exciting, sitting in Center Court and watching some of the best players in the world, before my junior games were scheduled.

The morning of my first round, I had a terrific surprise. There was Steve Casati, all the way from Chicago! He said, "I came to see you play Wimbledon, kid." It meant a lot to see another familiar face, someone else who knew how excited I was. "Besides," Steve said, "I want to make sure you remember all those drills we've worked on."

26

My first match was against a girl from Germany. I didn't feel jittery, just excited. Knowing Steve was there made me feel confident, and I thought it would be fun.

I won, 7-5, 6-4.

The next day, I won, too, even though the grass courts were
so slippery I fell once.

    The winner of the match after mine would be my opponent
in the quarterfinals, so Steve and I stayed and watched.
The girl who won was Isabel Villiger, from Switzerland.
Steve pointed out that she wouldn't win many points off her
backhand, but that she'd kill the ball hit high to her forehand.

Top players are "seeded," or ranked, for a tournament by how well they have been playing. Because I had so many wins that winter, I was seeded first at Junior Wimbledon. This meant I was supposed to have the best chance of winning—but it also meant I'd be the one everybody else wanted to beat.

On the way to my match, I thought about the Swiss girl, who was a strong player. I knew I would have to work hard to win. She had one advantage: she wasn't seeded, so she wasn't expected to win. She could just relax and go all out.

I got to Court Two early and watched the end of the match before mine. I tried to study the court so I'd know what to expect. Where were the bumps on the court? Where were the balls bouncing funny?

I also remembered that this court had been bad luck for seeded players all week.

Before our match began, Isabel Villiger and I met with the umpire. He explained the rules: We had ten minutes to warm up, and we could take one-minute breaks between court changes, and the first one to win two sets would be the winner of the match.

I spun my racquet to see who would serve first. Villiger won.

Villiger won the first game.
We changed sides on the court.

My serve.

I concentrated on aiming deep, to her backhand.

After our ten minutes' warm-up, we began play, Villiger serving.

The server always has an advantage, because she controls where the ball will land. On grass, it's especially important, because of the crazy way the balls bounce. It's much harder to anticipate your return shot.

We each won three games, but then I lost the next two. Villiger made some mistakes that gave me two points, but it hardly mattered. I was rushing every shot. Villiger took the first set, 6-4.

I didn't feel I had control of the ball. I decided to change racquets between sets. Maybe a racquet with looser tension in the strings would help.

Mom gets so nervous watching me, especially when I'm down a set. It's against the rules to coach a player, but I could almost hear Steve thinking, "C'mon, Andrea. Take charge."

Second set.

    I took a deep breath and walked back onto the court, telling myself, "Be aggressive, press more."

Changing racquets didn't seem to help. I knew Steve was wondering why I wasn't moving in, but I just didn't feel confident, and Villiger was keeping the ball deep. I had to quit thinking about the bumps on the court and start concentrating on hitting the ball.

I needed to pull ahead, but instead, I kept playing catch-up: 3–3...3–4...4–4...

At 4–5, my heart was pounding.
If I could win this game, I had a
chance to play another set. But
if she won, it was all over.

She returned my first serve
with a powerful forehand smash
down the line. I couldn't get
there. Stay away from her
forehand. You're serving to it
like it's a magnet. Her point.
Calm down, concentrate.

I served again. She slammed a hard return, but this time
into the net. My point. My next serve was perfect, deep into
the far backhand corner. It should have been a winner. But
Villiger returned with a slice that landed with a weird bounce.
Her point.

    I was so upset, I thought about that point and lost the next one.

Next I decided to move in after my serve and put her return away. It worked. My point.

I served. Villiger returned to my backhand. On the fourth hit, I smashed a forehand down the line...

Out!

Game, set, match to Villiger.

Losing hurt so much inside I barely managed to hold back the tears until I got off the court.

It had been a long time since I had lost an important match. I felt embarrassed, sad, and mad—all at the same time.

When I got back to the hotel, I called Susy in Texas and told her I had lost. She said, "Well, you think *you're* doing badly? Wait until you hear about *my* losses this week!" She started laughing, and pretty soon I was laughing, too. After that, I felt better.

I was anxious to get home, to start working on my game.

I planned on serving balls until I could hit that backhand court blindfolded. I'd do that baseline drill until my timing was perfect.

Next time I play at Wimbledon,
I'll be ready.

Afterword

After turning professional, Andrea Jaeger returned to
Wimbledon in 1980 as the youngest player ever seeded.
Ranked fourteenth she advanced all the way to the
quarterfinals of the tournament.